7 WAYS THE HOLY SPIRIT SPEAKS TO US

7 Ways the Holy Spirit Speaks to Us: A Complete Guide to Hearing God

Copyright © 2019 by Sean Pinder

All rights reserved solely by the author. The author guarantees all contents are original and do not infringe upon the legal rights of any other person or work. No part of this book may be reproduced in any form without the permission of the author. The views expressed in this book are not necessarily those of the publisher.

>Scripture quotations from The Authorized King James Version. Rights in the Authorized Version in the United Kingdom are vested in the Crown. Reproduced by permission of the Crown's patentee, Cambridge University Press.
>
>Scripture quotations marked (NLT) are taken from the Holy Bible, New Living Translation, copyright ©1996, 2004, 2015 by Tyndale House Foundation. Used by permission of Tyndale House Publishers, Inc., Carol Stream, Illinois 60188. All rights reserved.
>
>Scripture quotations marked MSG are taken from THE MESSAGE, copyright © 1993, 1994, 1995, 1996, 2000, 2001, 2002 by Eugene H. Peterson. Used by permission of NavPress. All rights reserved. Represented by Tyndale House Publishers, Inc.

ISBN-13: 9781688990722

Tall Pine Books: An Imprint of Pulpit to Page
|| tallpinebooks.com
|| pulpittopage.com

7 WAYS THE HOLY SPIRIT SPEAKS TO US

A COMPLETE GUIDE TO HEARING GOD

SEAN PINDER

TALL PINE

CONTENTS

Introduction   vii

PART I
THE METHODS

1. The Spirit's Grid   3
2. The Word   9
3. God's Servants   15
4. Dreams & Visions   21
5. Peace   31
6. Divine Impressions   37
7. Circumstances   43
8. The Still Small Voice   49

PART II
THE MOTIVATIONS

9. How to Be Sure It's a God Thing   55
10. The Danger of a Deaf Ear   65
11. Better to Be Safe than Sorry   71
12. Don't Lose Him!   77
13. King David's Greatest Fear   83
14. Christ, the Spirit, and You   87
15. Conclusion   95

Corresponding Chapter Questions   97
Meet the Author   105
Notes   107

INTRODUCTION

In 1993, I surrendered my life to Jesus. One night when I went to bed, I heard Jesus say, "Teach and then preach." I knew my job was to be a teacher, not merely a preacher. See, *preachers proclaim* whereas *teachers explain*. As a result, I pray that through this book, you'll experience the blessed exhortation of a preacher while at the same time drawing the key insights of a teacher. May this twofold grace cause you to be both encouraged and educated. May you be stirred up and instructed.

I have a specific goal for this book that you are reading: that God would use it to craft each reader into someone who is more mature, sensitive and quick to hear and obey the voice of the Holy Spirit. I truly feel that part of my mission in life is to communicate to the body of Christ that *every single believer can hear from God on a daily basis.*

To some, that might seem far fetched. Yet I would

ask, is there a parent that doesn't want to communicate with their child daily? God is so interested in communicating with us that He has given us a perfect guidebook through the scriptures in how to hear, interpret, and obey Him. Without regularly experiencing God's voice, we are desperately lacking.

Through this book, may you be given *confidence* to know that you are hearing God, *divine curiosity t*o lean in to hear His voice, and *hunger* to live a lifestyle of hearing and obeying God.

God is not short on words. In fact, He never has been short on words. Yet, I ask, *is He short on available listeners?* May our lives declare to Him that our ears are open, ready to hear His voice and to become the voice of God on this earth.

PART I

THE METHODS

If I want to get ahold of my wife, I can speak to her face to face, on the phone, or in a text. I could speak through my facial expressions, motion with my hands, use body language, or speak verbally. I could talk loud or I could whisper. There are varied methods available to us as we seek communication on a horizontal level with people. Likewise, there are varied methods available to us as we seek communication on a vertical level with God. In Part 1 of this book, we will take an in-depth look at the methods and means by which God speaks to us, His children.

1
THE SPIRIT'S GRID

A POWERFUL ANNOUNCEMENT WAS MADE AND RECORDED toward the end of the Gospel of John. Jesus Christ Himself was preparing to go back to Heaven. His earthly mission had wrapped up and without a doubt, His disciples were concerned. They likely had questions on their minds like, what's going to happen to us? Will we be left alone? There is no one like You, Lord...what will we do when you're gone? Fears about being left alone and being without help didn't end with the disciples. Many experience this same angst today. Jesus eased these worries with a statement that we can absolutely stake our lives on:

> "But the Comforter, which is the Holy Ghost, whom the Father will send in my name, He shall teach you all things, and bring all things to your remembrance, whatsoever I have said unto you." (John 14:26)

The language Christ uses is essential to understand. He calls the Holy Spirit the Comforter. The greek word for comforter is parakletos, which means strengthener, intercessor, teacher, advocate (like a lawyer to fight your case), and one called alongside to help.

How does He help exactly? Notice, Jesus said the Holy Ghost would be sent, "in My Name." Meaning, in My stead, in My place, and in My authority. He was making it very clear that the Holy Spirit would help by using His very words to bring guidance and direction to the disciples' lives. They wouldn't be without a compass, so to speak—and neither are we!

I remember when I used to say, "I wish Jesus were here physically!" I wanted to touch Him, be able to see Him, feel Him, and ask Him questions. Yet, we've been given One who has adequately taken on Jesus' ministry in the earth and He is the Holy Spirit.

Have you ever been doing something ordinary like driving your car, laying in bed, or washing dishes, and suddenly a scripture that you had read previously came up in your spirit? You weren't even thinking about the passage but suddenly it came alive and marked you! This is the Holy Spirit talking to you. Some people are praying, "Oh God, speak to me!" Yet the Lord is speaking by and through the word of God!

Have you ever been listening to a preacher and it feels as though he or she is speaking directly to you? You could be in a crowd of 500 but it feels like it's just you and the preacher. It's like he or she knows just what you're going through and they share a verse of scripture that brings comfort, understanding or breakthrough to your situation? This is the work of the Holy Spirit. The preacher doesn't know what you're dealing with or going through, yet God does.

Many of us have had those times where we've been confused, discouraged, beat down, at the end of our rope, and we hear a preacher and God moves through them—giving us exactly what we needed to hear. The yoke is destroyed and the burden is lifted. The Bible says, "When the enemy shall come in like a flood, the Spirit of the Lord shall lift up a standard against him" (Isaiah 59:19).

I can tell you many, many times we've found ourselves discouraged and downtrodden because of the enemy's flood, so to speak. Yet we've listened to a sermon and opened our Bibles and suddenly breakthrough happens. We find ourselves rejoicing, weeping and celebrating God's goodness. Why? Because we couldn't deny that God was speaking to us! Often, the standard that the Lord lifts up is His Spirit's voice through His holy word.

You know the voice of God better than you realize. Don't let the devil talk you out of it. Don't let people talk you out of it. Don't allow bad teaching to convince you that hearing God is an unattainable goal and that it's only for a select few. No, no, no; Jesus said, "My sheep hear my voice, and I know them, and they follow me" (John 10:27). If you are a blood-washed, born-again believer, you can hear the voice of the Lord. Let's examine some insight Jesus provides about the ministry of the Holy Spirit in John 16.

> "However when he, the Spirit of truth, is come, he will guide you into all truth: for he shall not speak of himself; but whatsoever he shall hear, that shall he speak: and he will shew you things to come." (John 16:13)

There are a few take-aways I want to draw your attention to in this passage.

- First, notice that Christ Jesus refers to Him as the Spirit of truth. This means He speaks truth and nothing but the truth. He cannot lie. If someone says, "God says such and such will happen," and it does not happen, then it was not of God, for God cannot lie.
- Second, notice that the Spirit, "shall not speak of himself," as the passage says. This means He speaks in the authority of Christ. There is no duplicity in the trinity. God is not a split personality. The Lord is one. The Holy Spirit directly communicates spiritually the same thing that Christ would communicate if He were here physically.
- Finally, the Lord highlights the prophetic nature of the Spirit by teaching, "he will shew you things to come." How so? Often, the Spirit

will take you through the scriptures and emphasize an event from the life of David, Paul, Timothy, Solomon or someone else and bring it alive in such a way that a biblical figure's testimony points to your future.

I can't tell you how many times that my wife and I have spent time in the word of God together and days later when we needed to make a specific decision, the Holy Ghost would remind us of the written word and we would know just what to do. You can trust the leading of the Holy Ghost! He will never lead you outside of the word of God.

When the enemy came against Jesus in Matthew 4 (also recorded in Luke 4), Jesus responded with the phrase, "It is written, Man shall not live by bread alone, but by every word that proceedeth out of the mouth of God" (Matthew 4:4 emphasis added). Psalm 33:4 declares, "For the word of the Lord is right..." David wrote later on, "Thy word is a lamp unto my feet, and a light unto my path" (Psalm 119:105).

The Holy Spirit holds up the written word of God and uses it like a flashlight as you walk down a dark street, showing you exactly where to step. The Holy Spirit will always lead you in line with the word of God. You can trust Him to do so. "Heaven and earth shall pass away, but my words shall not pass away" (Matthew 24:35). Flimsy prophecies from people will pass. The written word will not. Think of the word of God as the Holy

Spirit's grid. He won't leave the parameters of the word of God to speak to you. He operates within the boundaries of the word of God, giving direction and clarity to every facet of your life.

If there is ever a time that we need to be established in the word of God, it is in these last days that we are living in. We need to trust the work of the Holy Spirit in our lives! Everything that Jesus was to His disciples, the Holy Ghost is to you and I. The Spirit did not come as some mystical entity to sort of patch up the gaps that Christ's ascension left. No, the Holy Spirit came in a substitutionary way to continue and to expand the work and ministry of Jesus in this earth. As we lean into this reality, we'll begin to experience the rich benefit and blessing of life in the Spirit.

2

THE WORD

GOD'S GOLD STANDARD

"Every word of God is pure." (Proverbs 30:5)

The safest and most secure way to be led by the Spirit of God is through the written word of God. If you're going to be led by the Spirit in a safe and secure manner, you've got to be someone who spends time in the word. You've got to surround yourself with the scriptures, listen to men and women of God expound on the word, and be committed to educating yourself spiritually. The very fact that you are reading this book proves that you're on the right track and that you are hearing from God in the word.

The believer is called to be totally submerged in the word. Keep it in your heart. Keep it in your mind. Keep it in your eyes, in your mouth, and in your lifestyle. Look at David's solution to integrity and moral problems in the Psalms:

"Wherewithal shall a young man cleanse his way? By taking heed thereto according to thy word." (Psalm 119:9)

When folks get themselves into trouble, it is because they have stepped away from the word. People's marriages get into trouble because they've stepped out of the word. Folks get into trouble at their jobs, into trouble with the law, and into turmoil emotionally because they step out of the word. Even your prayer life takes a hit when you neglect the word of the living God:

"He that turneth away his ear from hearing the law (word), even his prayer shall be abomination." (Proverbs 28:9 parenthetical added)

Right after Joshua took over as Moses' successor, God gave him a piece of instruction before going about his exploits. He said to him, "This book of the law shall not depart out of thy mouth; but thou shalt meditate therein day and night, that thou mayest observe to do according to all that is written therein: for then thou shalt make thy way prosperous, and then thou shalt have good success" (Joshua 1:8).

Don't you know, it's the wisdom of God that makes you successful? I'm not talking about success based on the world's standards but success based on God's standard. In fact, when you put success first over the word of God...you end up with *no success*. Yet when you put the word of God first above success...you get both! Look at God's desire for us to prioritize His word:

> "The judgments (words) of the Lord are true and righteous altogether. More to be desired are they than gold, yea, than much fine gold: sweeter also than honey and the honeycomb. Moreover by them is thy servant warned: and in keeping of them there is great reward." (Psalm 19:9-11)

The word of God is the wisdom of God, the will of God and the very heartbeat of God. In fact, the word of God is God Himself! "In the beginning was the Word, and the Word was with God, and the Word was God" (John 1:1). The chapter goes on to say, "And the Word was made flesh, and dwelt among us" (John 1:14).

The Holy Spirit takes the word of God and by it, reveals to us the nature of God. The word represents who God is because the word is who God is. The mind, voice and heart of God come through the word. In this, we are not without wisdom concerning our children, ministries, marriages, and our lives as a whole. To say, "I'm going to hear the voice of God," and totally neglect the Bible is a great error.

We need to get back to the word of God. Trust that the Holy Spirit will teach you line upon line, precept upon precept (see Isaiah 28:10). He will lead you in the direction you ought to go. Of course, when I'm referring to being led, I'm not talking about being led by dreams.

Although, I do believe that some dreams are from God and of course, some dreams are not, which we'll talk about in a later chapter. Likewise, I believe some prophecies spoken by people are of God, and others are straight flesh and nonsense. I want you to catch this, friends, if you don't know the word of God, you won't be able to accurately judge a prophetic word as being from God. Knowing the written word of God literally sets you up to properly judge the spoken word of God through man. Catch this: the written voice of God postures you to clearly hear and judge the prophetic voice of God through people.

In Colossians, Paul gives us insight to being led by the Lord. He said, "Let the word of Christ dwell in you richly in all wisdom; teaching and admonishing one another in psalms and hymns and spiritual songs, singing with grace in your hearts to the Lord" (Colossians 3:16). Did you catch that? He said, "Let the word of Christ dwell in you richly." Meaning, the guiding path of God's voice is the scriptures. I don't want just any person off the street to lay hands on me and prophesy over me. I want the word of God to give me the direction that I hunger for.

If someone gives you a prophecy that runs against the word of God...take that prophecy and throw it in the garbage. The Holy Spirit will never speak anything that is contrary to the written word. Beware of parking lot prophets who wait until service is out to leave the authority of the pastor and the service to prophesy and blab over you to impress you or entertain you. God is a God of order. The Bible is our plumb line and the standard bearer, keeping us centered and on track. This gold standard keeps us balanced and steady as we endeavor to hear and obey the voice of the Spirit.

3
GOD'S SERVANTS
WHEN PEOPLE BECOME GOD'S MOUTHPIECE

GOD SPEAKS TO US THROUGH HIS SERVANTS. HE DID through Isaiah, Jeremiah, Elijah, Elisha, John, Peter, Paul and more. Listen, God is still speaking through His servants today. Divine communication through human vessels did not stop when the scriptures were canonized. No, the voice of God through man has continued. Bear in mind, it's not the only way that God speaks to us—but it is one of the primary ways God speaks to us.

When a person is under the unction of the Holy Spirit, the voice of God will come to them in a strong way. As you sit under their teaching, you'll hear the very voice of God coming through the message. As a result, He will bring healing, wisdom, knowledge and understanding. Your relationship with Jesus will go to another level if you are sitting under a true man or woman of God. You'll fall deeper in love with Jesus and experience more of His will in your life, if you adhere to God's plan to receive from His voice through His servants.

You don't want someone to tickle your ear or share a weak message inspired by the flesh. You want someone to *come clean with you*, so to speak, and authentically communicate the Lord's heart. Of course, the same standards apply when hearing a sermon; if what a preacher is saying doesn't agree with the word of God...the sermon didn't come from God.

In the scriptures, we see a great story of victory in the life of King Jehoshaphat. He was reigning as king over Israel and opposing nations attempted to destroy and annihilate their land. Jehoshaphat made a wise move and called his people to fast and pray. As they prayed and cried out to the Lord, look at what happened:

> "Then upon Jahaziel the son of Zechariah, the son of Benaiah, the son of Jeiel, the son of Mattaniah, a Levite of the sons of Asaph, came the Spirit of the Lord in the midst of the congregation. And he said, Hearken ye, all Judah, and ye inhabitants of Jerusalem, and thou king Jehoshaphat, Thus saith the Lord unto you, Be not afraid nor dismayed by reason of this great multitude; for the battle is not yours, but God's." (2 Chronicles 20:14-15)

The Spirit of God came into the midst of the situation and when He did, He didn't just hang out or give folks goosebumps. He spoke through the man of God

Jahaziel! Jahaziel opened his mouth with a word inspired by the Lord and declared that which God was declaring. The people were distressed, fearful, uncertain, and weary—yet the real word of the Lord brought an answer to the situation and encouragement in the time of need. The real word of God spoken through His servant brings:

- Comfort
- Peace
- Direction
- Correction
- Discipline
- Encouragement
- Breakthrough

Jahaziel said, this battle is not yours but God's. What a relief that is! This means that you are more than a conqueror. You're coming out the head and not the tail. You are the *victor* and not the *victim*. You are above and not beneath. You're blessed coming in, blessed going out, blessed in the city, and blessed in the field!

It's working together for your good because you love God and are called according to His purpose. You're coming out of the bondage you've been in. You're coming out of the trial. Look at the example of our King. They crucified Him in cold blood. He was buried in a borrowed tomb. For three days He laid there. Yet on the third day the power of the Holy Ghost descended and an angel moved the stone out of the way and God brought Jesus out of the grave.

I'm here to tell you that the stone has rolled away in your life. Nothing shall be impossible! You have the same Spirit that raised Christ from the dead within you! Victory is yours. The devil meant the attack for evil in your life, *but God is working it out for your good!*

No weapon that is formed against you will be able to prosper! Every tongue that rises against you in judgment will be condemned. It was Jesus who said, "Upon this rock I will build my church and the gates of hell shall not prevail against it" (see Matthew 16). The Bible declares that when the enemy comes against you, the Spirit of God will raise up a standard against him!

Many are the afflictions of the righteous but the Lord delivers him out of them all (see Psalm 34). Maybe you're going through trials, tribulations, and hard times. Perhaps you're like Jehoshaphat, and you feel pressured on every side. You've been under attack and it seems there is no way out. Yet I believe the Holy Ghost has sent me to tell you that the Lord will deliver you out of this. In the same way that Jahaziel declared by the Spirit that the battle is not yours but God's, I declare the same thing to you today!

The snare of the devil is broken and you can escape! Your help is in the name of the Lord which made the heavens and the earth! The name of the Lord is a strong tower! The righteous will run into it and be safe. Even when you walk through the valley of the shadow of death, you will fear no evil for God is with you. God is on your side. Why should you fear what man can do to you? Look to the hills from where your help comes! Your help comes from the Lord!

Believe these things! Claim these things in your life. When you do, you are allowing yourself to be encouraged, inspired, uplifted, changed, and challenged by the voice of God speaking through man. When I write these things, I'm not offering Christian-hype and I'm not trying to give you a little fleshly pep talk. No, I am offering you the principles and promises of the eternal, living God! Make no mistake about it, many people fail to enjoy the blessed benefit of the voice of God through man because they write it off or pay no attention. One might read the encouragement I've given and say, "Yeah but that's not for me." As a result, they miss the very direct, personal voice of God coming at them. Yet, I want you to know that God is still using people to communicate His truths and if you'll open yourself to these avenues, you'll reap the benefits and walk in a new measure of freedom and victory in your life.

4

DREAMS & VISIONS
VISUALS OF A HEAVENLY ORIGIN

AT THE VERY START OF THE NEW TESTAMENT, WE SEE THE nativity story of the birth of Jesus. At the time of His birth, Herod was seeking to find and kill baby Jesus. Yet he could not kill what God had begun until it was time for Christ's sufferings to commence.

> "And being warned of God in a dream that they should not return to Herod, they departed into their own country another way. And when they were departed, behold, the angel of the Lord appeareth to Joseph in a dream, saying, Arise, and take the young child and his mother, and flee into Egypt, and be thou there until I bring thee word: for Herod will seek the young child to destroy him." (Matthew 2:12-13)

The wise men who offered gifts and sacrifices to the Lord Jesus were warned in a dream not to return to

Herod but to go another route. Isn't that awesome? While we are sound asleep, God will give us instructions. This is how much He loves us. Not only does the Lord warn the wise men through a dream but He directs Joseph in a dream.

When the message is important, the Lord will see to it that it is communicated in a manner that is beyond obscurity and misunderstanding. Joseph had a dream of direction and knew he needed to hide the infant Messiah in Egypt until further notice.

Don't you know that God knows just where to hide you from the enemy? The famous scripture declares, "He that dwelleth in the secret place of the most High shall abide under the shadow of the Almighty. I will say of the Lord, He is my refuge and my fortress: my God; in Him will I trust. Surely he shall deliver thee from the snare of the fowler, and from the noisome pestilence.

He shall cover thee with his feathers, and under his wings shalt thou trust: his truth shall be thy shield and buckler. Thou shalt not be afraid for the terror by night; nor for the arrow that flieth by day; Nor for the pestilence that walketh in darkness; nor for the destruction that wasteth at noonday. A thousand shall fall at thy side, and ten thousand at thy right hand; but it shall not come nigh thee" (Psalm 91:1-7).

Not only does a dream occur to instruct Joseph to hide out in Egypt but a follow up dream occurs later on as the scriptures describe:

"But when Herod was dead, behold, an angel of the Lord appeareth in a dream to Joseph in Egypt, Saying, Arise, and take the young child and his mother, and go into the land of Israel: for they are dead which sought the young child's life. And he arose, and took the young child and his mother, and came into the land of Israel. But when he heard that Archelaus did reign in Judaea in the room of his father Herod, he was afraid to go thither: notwithstanding, being warned of God in a dream, he turned aside into the parts of Galilee: And he came and dwelt in a city called Nazareth: that it might be fulfilled which was spoken by the prophets, He shall be called a Nazarene." (Matthew 2:19-23)

We see even in the life of Jesus as a baby, God was warning His earthly parents and communicating with them via dreams. These dreams brought about divine protection for the Child. There are various ways that dreams and visions come to us. It may happen while you are conscious, which we refer to as an open vision. It may happen while asleep at night, which would be a dream of the night. Either way, when these things happen, they always produce positive fruit of protection and wholeness when we act on them appropriately.

I remember sitting in a service in McKinney, Texas, visiting a pastor friend of mine. While the service was going and worship was happening, all of a sudden, I began to have an open vision. In the vision, I saw a man at the far left side of the church. I saw myself calling him out and saying to him, "You have been having problems with your back and the Holy Spirit wants to heal you right now." I saw myself calling him forward and laying hands on him and he was instantly healed by God's power.

I had never seen this man before in my life. The vision came out of the blue. So I craned my neck and looked to the back of the church and sure enough, the man was standing there. I said to the Lord, "OK, You have shown me what to do, Lord. Have the pastor call me up to do what You have asked me to do." It's not proper protocol to just take over a pastor's service just because you had a vision. God works through proper channels of authority and structure.

Sure enough, the pastor stood up and turned to me and said, "Pastor Sean, would you stand up and greet the people and pray for some of them?" You don't have to guess who I prayed for first! I stood up and looked at the back of the church and called out the man from my vision. I said, "You have problems in your back and the Lord wants to heal you." Sure enough, it was spot-on and he came forward to be healed. It happened just as it did in the vision. The only thing I had to do was obey what I saw in the vision.

My wife and I have experienced many dreams and visions from the Lord over the course of time. Some are urgent, some are warnings, some are prophetic and some are words of knowledge and pieces of information in a service, for example, to bless and benefit people in the congregation. Regardless of their purpose, it is important to recognize that you cannot force these things to take place. You ought to never fabricate a dream or a vision. Don't make the mistake of hearing a man or woman of God talk about their dreams and visions and pretend that you've got to go make these things happen for yourself. No, they happen in the Lord's timing. God is not a man that He should lie. If He has spoken to you through a dream or vision, you can bet that it will come to pass with certainty. Don't lose heart and do not give up.

> "For the vision is yet for an appointed time, but at the end it shall speak, and not lie: though it tarry, wait for it; because it will surely come, it will not tarry." (Habakuk 2:3)

Discernment & Accountability

Not every dream and not every vision is a God-dream or a God-vision. You can tell when a dream or vision is from the devil because it brings an evil presence with it. When that happens you need to stand up and rebuke that thing! Don't just accept any and every dream as being from the Lord. Satan would love to give you false dreams of catastrophe and destruction to you and your family. Get up and bind those things in the name of Jesus. If the vision is causing a fear that is not the fear of the Lord, don't adhere to it! Don't accept it.

Not only that, but some dreams are just dreams. They might be night-time regurgitation of something that happened that day. Some are "pizza dreams" as they call them and have no spiritual value or meaning at all. There's no need to spend hours journaling and seeking prophetic counsel over dreams that were just your imagination. However, when a dream is of the Lord, lean in!

When Daniel had received revelation from the Lord about Nebuchadnezzar's dream, Daniel was praising God and giving Him honor. He knew what to do with it. There was clarity, peace, and an answer involved. Likewise, our dreams and visions ought to produce clear fruit in our midst and in the lives of those around us. If you ever have questions or concerns about whether or not something is of God, leverage your relationships with solid leaders in your life to find accountability and strength.

> "Now when they had gone throughout Phrygia and the region of Galatia, and were forbidden of the Holy Ghost to preach the word in Asia." (Acts 16:6)

Paul was going about his ministry and was checked in his spirit by the Holy Ghost. In modern terms, we might say, "I felt like I didn't have a green light to move forward." Many of us have experienced this before. We've felt as though we didn't have the Lord's permission to move forward with something. There was an internal knowing and a hesitancy in our spirit. That is the Holy Spirit getting our attention!

Friends, many men have married the wrong woman and many women have married the wrong man because they ignored the check in their spirit. Folks have pushed aside red flags because they got caught up in emotion and became trapped by what they wanted to do. As a result, they end up in an absolute mess. Meanwhile, God was trying to pull on them and warn them the whole time. The same thing is true over jobs to take, moves to make and many other arenas of life.

In my own life, I have felt God put a check in my spirit over various matters and I've pushed it aside only to do my own thing. As a result, I've paid a price. I'm not trying to do that again! It's best to yield to the Spirit's leading and avoid what He calls you to avoid.

As we read, Paul was forbidden to preach in Asia. There's nothing wrong with preaching the word. He was called to do so, in fact. Yet if he would have forged ahead, he would have been out of the will of God. It wasn't the right timing and it wasn't the right territory. The right thing at the wrong time is still wrong. Let's continue:

> "After they were come to Mysia, they assayed to go into Bithynia: but the Spirit suffered them not." (Acts 16:7)

They wanted to go to Bithynia, but the Spirit forbid them to do so. Friends, that is a safe place to be. After they had twice obeyed the warning of the Spirit, God directed their path with a green light:

> "And they passing by Mysia came down to Troas. And a vision appeared to Paul in the night; There stood a man of Macedonia, and prayed him, saying, Come over into Macedonia, and help us. And after he had seen the vision, immediately we endeavored to go into Macedonia, assuredly gathering that the Lord had called us for to preach the gospel unto them." (Acts 16:8-10)

Luke, the doctor, is writing these verses. Notice that he said they all endeavored to to go into Macedonia because they all concurred that the Lord called them to preach there. Paul had the vision, brought it to his colleagues for accountability's sake, and they all agreed that the vision was of God.

Listen, if you have a vision—don't just jump up and act on it immediately. Study the Bible. Search the scriptures to find confirmation. Talk to a seasoned pastor or leader to bounce it off of them. Dreams and visions are one of the most misconstrued and misappropriated means of hearing God, the reason being that people can hide or get lost in ambiguity. If the Apostle Paul submitted his vision to be scrutinized by those he was with, don't you think that you and I should submit our visions to those around us for counsel and confirmation? The scripture says, "Where no counsel is, the people fall:

but in the multitude of counsellors there is safety" (Proverbs 11:14).

The word safety in this passage means that God will give you victory through human instruments. God will use people in your midst to solidify that which He has spoken to you. By taking these measures, you will avoid deception and remain in the will of God because you've adhered to the voice of God by observing the proper methods of God.

by sight! Let God's spoken voice in your spirit speak louder than external conditions.

I have folks that write to me all the time wanting me to make decisions for them. I am not going to make decisions for you. That's not my role. You have the Holy Spirit. You know what to do internally. The Spirit lives in you. Some folks want me to say something that confirms some crazy decision for them that is outside of the will of God, yet I won't do that. I will point you back to listening to the Holy Spirit for yourself and learning to sense the peace of God or a lack of the peace of God on a situation or decision.

Many miss these things because they want God to speak to them in some grandiose, sensational fashion. They want big writing in the sky to appear, telling them what to do. Listen, God might not speak to you in the way you want Him to speak to you, but He speaks to you in the way that you need to be spoken to. The peace of God is one of the most common ways that the Lord directs His children and we've got to mature into a place in which we recognize it and adhere to it!

If you are out there seeking after audible voices and sensational happenings you can be deceived. Does God speak in those sensational ways and audibly to His people? Absolutely! But that doesn't mean that it should be the method we chase? We *don't chase methods*. We *adhere to the word*. The word encourages us to be *ruled by peace in all our decisions and exploits.*

"Furthermore, when I came to Troas to preach Christ's gospel, and a door was opened unto me of the Lord, I had no rest in my spirit, because I found not Titus my brother: but taking my leave of them, I went from thence into Macedonia." (2 Corinthians 2:12-13)

Notice, Paul said that he had restlessness in his spirit. Even though there was an open door for him to do ministry, the relational situation with Titus was out of whack causing his heart to be restless rather than at peace. A similar restlessness took place in my life recently. My wife and I almost bought the wrong house. We had felt good about it and even thought we had a peace about it for a time. The devil will certainly give a false sense of calm in order to trip up our decision making.

Yet when we really pressed into prayer and heard from the Lord, we were unsettled in our spirit and didn't pull the trigger on what would have been a bad investment. Proverbs declares a famous truth that we ought to guard in our hearts, "Trust in the Lord with all thine heart; and lean not unto thine own understanding. In all thy ways acknowledge him, and he shall direct thy paths" (Proverbs 3:5-6).

"When Jesus had thus said, he was troubled in spirit, and testified, and said, Verily, verily, I say unto you, that one of you shall betray me." (John 13:21)

Now why was Jesus troubled in his spirit? We find out a few moments later in verse 27 that, "Satan entered into him [Judas]." When you begin to feel troubled about someone in your life and you start to see attitudes and actions that don't reflect the nature of God—you need to pay attention. It's possible that the devil himself has entered into the conversation. I don't mean to be a broken record, but if you're being troubled, put the brakes on! Bounce decisions off of leaders in your life. The word troubled in the previous passage means:

Troubled: to agitate, to cause one inward commotion, to take away the calmness of mind, to disturb, to disquiet, to make restless, to stir up, to strike one's spirit with fear and dread, to render anxiety or distress, to perplex the mind by suggesting scruples and doubts.

God will bring a troubling in your spirit if someone in your life is getting off track. It will enable you to be watchful, careful and prayerful as you move forward. Your intercession for them can pull them back on track. However, in some cases, like Judas, they don't come back on track. Regardless, you've got to pay attention when you are troubled about a person you are in relationship with. If they have opened the door to the devil in their lives and you have opened the door to them when you shouldn't have, you also are opening the door to the devil. These things ought not be! When people change for the worse and begin to stray, you've got to catch it.

Just recently we were feeling some uneasiness toward certain relationships and we watched a powerful message from a seasoned man of God who has been preaching the gospel and walking with Jesus for over 50 years. His teaching confirmed everything that we had been feeling and encouraged us to be watchful. Some call it, "Having a bad feeling in your gut." Some call it, "Sensing trouble." Regardless of what you call it, if a situation, relationship or scenario in your life gives you pause and you feel uneasy—trust the Lord and obey His leading. Peace is the hallmark of a God inspired decision. Don't go without it!

6

DIVINE IMPRESSIONS

SUBTLE AND SURE LEADINGS

"I have also spoken by the prophets, and I have multiplied visions, and used similitudes, by the ministry of the prophets." (Hosea 12:10)

NOW, THE PASSAGE STATES THAT GOD HAS SPOKEN BY prophets and then proceeds to show how. We've covered visions, as the scripture above mentions. But I want to focus on that word similitudes. This word in the original Hebrew language means *images in the mind*. The Lord will show you things by pressing images into your mind. Any time I sense the Lord pressing someone on my mind really strong, I know it's a signal to pray for that person or call them up. So many times I have had folks on my mind for weeks and suddenly that person calls me up and needs prayer or a word of encouragement.

How many times have you had someone or something on your mind and you have thought, why am I thinking about this or that so much lately? And you thought that it was just you but it turned out to be from God? When you thought it was just your mind, it turned out to be the Lord transposing His thoughts with your thoughts. We often experience this but don't recognize it as God. We, in fact, have a variety of names we use to describe it, such as:

- A Hunch
- Instinct
- A Sensing
- A Knowing
- An Unction
- An Urge

Often, these things all describe the subtle impressions that God gives in order to direct our actions, prayer lives, relationships and ministries. I want to visit the book of Daniel for a moment to look at an Old Testament example of these impressions being made manifest:

> "But there is a God in heaven that revealeth secrets, and maketh known to the king Nebuchadnezzar what shall be in the latter days. Thy dream, and the visions of thy head upon thy bed, are these; As for thee, O king, thy thoughts came into thy mind upon thy bed, what should come to pass hereafter: and he that

revealeth secrets maketh known to thee what shall come to pass." (Daniel 2:28-29)

Did you catch that? He said, "thy thoughts came into thy mind." What are thoughts? Mental conceptions that you see in your mind. Another definition is, an idea produced by thinking, or occurring suddenly in the mind. Daniel was given divine interpretations through thoughts coming to mind. Many folks want to remove the mind from the equation when hearing from God yet God speaks into our minds! Don't buy into the idea that God only speaks to our spirits. If our minds are not involved, then we will fail to comprehend and understand what God is speaking.

When we are hosting a miracle service or doing a live broadcast, I will often call out a sickness or ailment that I see in someone who is watching or someone in the congregation. Often, this comes from an impression. A thought enters that is so strong, I know it cannot be of myself. Sometimes we can tell that something is off with people who are close to us because we sense and see what they are wrestling with and what they are going through. These impressions are not to be neglected or written off as being merely from ourselves. Learn to recognize when God Himself has planted His thoughts in our imaginations!

Let me give you an example of this from the very life of Christ:

"Nathanael saith unto him, Whence knowest thou me? Jesus answered and said unto him, Before that Philip called thee, when thou wast under the fig tree, I saw thee. Nathanael answered and saith unto him, Rabbi, thou art the Son of God; thou art the King of Israel. Jesus answered and said unto him, Because I said unto thee, I saw thee under the fig tree, believest thou? thou shalt see greater things than these." (John 1:48-50)

Wow! How did Jesus see things that Nathanael was doing before they even connected? In Christ's mind, He saw this ahead of time. He got Nathanael's name, even. And what was the fruit of the experience? Nathanael declared the Lordship of Christ and took note of the Messiah as being from God!

Take note of the impressions, images, pictures, nudges, and flashes that the Lord brings before your mind's eye. They might last for a moment or they might be pressed into your thinking repeatedly over time. In the same way that we can get better at a sport, an instrument, or a language—we can get better at recognizing these impressions.

We certainly aren't born into the kingdom with an automatic, perfect ability to catch all of these impressions. Like with anything else in our walk with God, we have room to grow and improve. Sensitivity can be developed over time as you lean in and grow in your awareness of the Spirit's presence in your daily life. As you take note of these impressions, you will see beautiful fruit showing up as a result of heeding them.

7
CIRCUMSTANCES
EVENTS THAT TALK

You've got to understand that the seasons of our lives change. Ecclesiastes talks about how for everything under heaven, there is a season and a time. Sometimes, we are not as attentive to the Holy Spirit as we should be and as a result, God speaks through circumstances. Other times, He begins to change the circumstances of our lives without giving us advance notice because frankly, our permission is not needed.

He will change the season that we are in, and perhaps we didn't even see it coming. We see the seasons change in nature as the leaves become red, brown, and yellow and eventually fall off through the autumn and winter months. Likewise, seasons change in our jobs, lives, ministries and ventures. The Lord sometimes brings about these shifts and we see and hear His voice in the midst of it.

When seasons change, don't fight it—flow with it!

For example, in scripture, God had to snatch Joseph away from his family to teach him how to trust the Lord. Joseph was becoming too dependent on his parents. Had he stayed there, God wouldn't have been able to do what He wanted to do with him. Often, the Lord will call us out, move us, and transition us in order to bring about His purposes in our lives. God said, "Behold, I will do a new thing; now it shall spring forth; shall ye not know it?" (Isaiah 43:19). Oftentimes we know and see the new thing that He is doing because our circumstances begin to change and shift to align with the will of God.

Let's have a look at an example of circumstances declaring God's voice in the Bible:

> "And the word of the Lord came unto him, saying, Get thee hence, and turn thee eastward, and hide thyself by the brook Cherith, that is before Jordan. And it shall be, that thou shalt drink of the brook; and I have commanded the ravens to feed thee there. So he went and did according unto the word of the Lord: for he went and dwelt by the brook Cherith, that is before Jordan. And the ravens brought him bread and flesh in the morning, and bread and flesh in the evening; and he drank of the brook."

The ravens began bringing provision to Elijah. It was the first fast food delivery service in history! He had bread, meat, and water in the river. He was being spoiled! Yet a shift took place:

"And it came to pass after a while, that the brook dried up because there had been no rain in the land. And the word of the Lord came unto him, saying, Arise, get thee to Zarephath, which belongeth to Zidon, and dwell there: behold, I have commanded a widow woman there to sustain thee." (1 Kings 17:2-9)

As soon as the brook dried up and his fast food delivery service stopped, Elijah knew something was happening. God was getting his attention. Listen, when your brook dries up and circumstances begin to change, you've got to find out what God is saying in the midst of it! Now, when I talk about your brook drying up I'm not talking about some demonic attack or an assault that is against the will of God in your life. I'm just referring to seasons shifting and supply that is normally present organically, by the will of God, begins to wane. Perhaps finances start to dry up in a certain area and you know that it's time to go about another venture. The Lord will allow these things to happen circumstantially in order for us to stop and hear His voice in the midst of it.

Sometimes this looks like God stripping your life bare because He is about to do a new thing that is beyond your imagination. Sometimes it looks like people leaving your life and new folks showing up. For some of you reading this, you've had these seasons shifting and God is trying to speak to you. Maybe you lost a job and the Lord is launching you into your own enterprise. Maybe people have left your life and new folks have entered because you're about to be brought into mind-blowing kingdom partnerships. Let go of the old season. Embrace the new. You might not understand it but you don't have to! Let the Lord launch you. He knows exactly what it is that He is doing.

Some time ago, we lived in a home and for a season it seemed like everything was going wrong with it. We'd fix one thing and then something else would break. We'd patch that up and then another part of the home would have issues. It was one thing after another. Then we recognized, the Lord was trying to get us out of there!

We discerned it correctly and the Lord confirmed it. Our brook was drying up. It was time to move on. God had something better in mind for us! If something in your life isn't meeting your needs, it's because God is shifting you into a new season of *better*. It's your season of increase. It's your season to step into the newness. He is speaking through circumstances. Walk through the door He opens. Your job might be drying up but the Lord might be trying to give you a job where you are a supervisor making four times as much! Perhaps the home is failing because the Lord is trying to move you to a new and better home in a better zip code! Your season of lack is ending. A season of abundance is coming!

The word says, "You faithfully answer our prayers with awesome deeds..." (Psalm 65:5 NLT). I want you to focus on the fact that it says He answers "with awesome deeds." What are deeds? They are *actions*. Sometimes, God doesn't answer our prayers verbally but with action.

He just begins to move and shift things and cause circumstances to change.

In Mark 4, we see a story of Jesus and the disciples crossing the lake during a ministry trip. A storm arises and things go haywire. Jesus is sleeping peacefully. The disciples panic and cry out, "Master, carest thou not that we perish?" (Mark 4:38). The Bible doesn't even record that Jesus answered them verbally. It simply says, "And he arose, and rebuked the wind, and said unto the sea, Peace, be still. And the wind ceased, and there was a great calm" (Mark 4:39).

Of course, He spoke to them after the fact. But at first, He simply answered their prayer with action! He *changed the circumstances!* Keep your eyes and ears open to the voice of God through circumstances and seasons being altered by the hand of God Almighty.

8

THE STILL SMALL VOICE

HEARING DIVINE WHISPERS

GOD DOESN'T ALWAYS TALK LOUDLY. OFTEN, IT IS A STILL, small voice that requires our leaning into hear Him. We must lean in as He leads. The still small voice is so gentle and soft that we must be careful to not miss it. Think about the way that a husband and wife communicate, for example. At times it may be with louder volume and more clear expressions but at other times, it may be a whisper or in a more gentle voice and tone. Likewise, the Bridegroom sometimes speaks to His bride, the church, with still whispers that require a fine-tuned ear to hear. Let's examine again, what Christ has said on the topic:

> "And when he putteth forth his own sheep, he goeth before them, and the sheep follow him: for they know his voice. And a stranger will they not follow, but will flee from him: for they know not the voice of strangers." (John 10:4-5)

We shouldn't think it strange that the Lord would want to talk to us. After all, Paul said, "What? know ye not that your body is the temple of the Holy Ghost which is in you, which ye have of God, and ye are not your own?" (1 Corinthians 6:19) Of course such nearness will result in us hearing the voice of the Lord! He lives in us! Let's have a look at one of the more famous passages on the still, small voice of God:

> "And he said, Go forth, and stand upon the mount before the Lord. And, behold, the Lord passed by, and a great and strong wind rent the mountains, and break in pieces the rocks before the Lord; but the Lord was not in the wind: and after the wind an earthquake; but the Lord was not in the earthquake: And after the earthquake a fire; but the Lord was not in the fire: and after the fire a still small voice.
>
> And it was so, when Elijah heard it, that he wrapped his face in his mantle, and went out, and stood in the entrance of the cave. And, behold, there came a voice unto him, and said, What doest thou here, Elijah?" (1 Kings 19:11-13)

Elijah had slain the prophets of Baal. Jezebel, an evil, demonic woman had been after him and it was a tumultuous season of life. Notice, the Lord was not in the wind, or the earthquake. He was not in the fire or the dramatic, loud events. Instead, He was in the still small voice. How many times have you been about to do something and you heard a subtle voice tell you to not do something? This was the subtle, quiet voice of the Holy Spirit. We see another example of this in Acts:

> "As they ministered to the Lord, and fasted, the Holy Ghost said, Separate me Barnabas and Saul for the work whereunto I have called them. And when they had fasted and prayed, and laid their hands on them, they sent them away. So they, being sent forth by the Holy Ghost, departed unto Seleucia; and from thence they sailed to Cyprus." (Acts 13:2-4)

It was the Holy Spirit who gave Paul and Barnabus direction as to where to go next. Their ministry was successful! I want to call your attention to an important detail in this story. The word says, "As they ministered to the Lord..." Ministry to the Lord positions you to hear and adhere to the subtle, small voice of God. It didn't say that they were tapping their feet, waiting around, hoping to gain direction. No, they were certainly lifting their voice, worshipping, and giving honor to God. This creates the ideal atmosphere for the still, small voice of God to be heard.

Not only did they minister to the Lord, but they fasted. They turned their plates upside down, so to speak. They prayed. They pressed in. It brought them to a place where the flesh was subdued and they could hear the voice of the Spirit. When we minister to the Lord, fast, and pray—it quiets other noises so the quiet voice of the Holy Ghost can be heard. We are swept into the arena of the Spirit. Our sensitivity to the Lord increases dramatically. This is why we start our services and broadcasts with worship and ministry to the Lord. It postures us to hear God with more clarity and sensitivity. Even before I read my Bible in the mornings, I adore the Lord and give Him worship.

This is so much better than reducing prayer to just, "Lord I need this and I need that. Amen." It's time to grow up! It's time to grow into a place of maturity. Turn off nonsense television. Get rid of garbage music in your life. It is clogging your receptors so that you cannot hear the subtle voice of God. Come out from among them and be separate! God is expecting much from us. Train your spirit man to be sensitive to the Lord.

Get alone with God. Shut the world out. Lock yourself away for a time to pray and seek the Lord. He will avail His voice to you in ways you've never experienced before. Why does He speak softly? So we are required to *lean in*. He shouldn't have to always speak with a booming, loud voice. Sensitive followers of Jesus are ready and available to hear those subtle utterances.

PART II

THE MOTIVATIONS

As you may well know, the mere *methods* of God are not *fully* experienced until we recognize the *motivations* of God. We've seen that God speaks and directs in a variety of manners, yet the reasons for His speaking are of utmost importance. In part 2 of this book, I want to explore topics that will help to highlight your dire need to fellowship with the Spirit, hear the Spirit, and thereby *obey* the Spirit.

9
HOW TO BE SURE IT'S A GOD THING

WHEN THERE ARE THREE DOORS OPEN IN FRONT OF YOU, how do you know which door to walk through? Are there guidelines in the word of God to help us understand when to say yes and when to say no? When picking the door to open, how do you know you are making the right decision? But most importantly, how do you know you are making the *God-inspired decision?* In his letter to the Romans, the Apostle Paul clues us in on how to navigate these decisions:

> "For as many as are led by the Spirit of God, they are the sons of God. For ye have not received the spirit of bondage again to fear; but ye have received the Spirit of adoption, whereby we cry, Abba, Father. The Spirit itself beareth witness with our spirit, that we are the children of God." (Romans 8:14-16)

From the day you accepted Jesus Christ as your Lord and Savior, the Spirit of God came to live inside of you. Jesus confirmed this by saying, "But ye know him (the Spirit); for he dwelleth with you, and shall be in you" (John 14:17 parenthetical/emphasis added). Paul spoke of these same realities, "What? know ye not that your body is the temple of the Holy Ghost which is in you, which ye have of God, and ye are not your own?" (1 Corinthians 6:19)

It would be worth just repeating out loud: the Spirit of God lives inside of me! Say it a few times, even. Why? Because you must develop a consciousness that the Spirit of God lives in you 24/7. He doesn't take a break. He is always there. He doesn't pack up and leave for a vacation. He doesn't flee when things get rough in your life. He is ever available, and ever present—not just near you but in you.

The word *led* in the passage above means, *to lead one by laying hold of them or to bring them to the point of their destination.* It also means *to attach oneself to someone as an attendant or to direct through the influence of the mind.* These are God's positions in our lives through the Holy Spirit.

From the scripture we read, we draw the conclusion that the way the Holy Spirit leads us is by bearing witness to us, or as some translations say, He testifies to us. To testify means to corroborate by evidence. The Holy Spirit uses the evidence of the word of God to testify to you of the will of God in any given situation.

Notice, the passage said, "As many as are led by the Spirit of God, they are the sons of God." It didn't say, "As many as are led by the man of God, these are the sons of God." Many modern Christians are stuck in an Old Testament mindset when it comes to being led by God. What do I mean by this?

What I mean is that in the Old Covenant, prophets were mediators between the voice of God in very directional and authoritative ways. If one wanted to hear from God, they had to go to a prophet, generally speaking. Yet now, the function of a prophet has changed. All believers have the ability to hear the voice of God. By simply reading and digesting scriptures, you won't be able to help but hear God as you move ahead! He is on assignment to keep you, preserve you, lead you and equip you to keep you on track!

I am sure you use the GPS on your phone. I love my GPS. Even when you know just where to go, it's good to keep your GPS on as it will inform you of wrecks ahead, road construction, or potential bottlenecks and congested areas in your route. As a result, the GPS will redirect you accordingly.

The GPS only speaks up when a turn is needed or a re-routing should take place. At that moment, you know to listen to the GPS as it has information that you do not. As a result, it saves you trouble and time! Likewise in our walk with Jesus, He will speak to our hearts during critical moments to save us time, trouble, headache and heartache. He knows not merely what to communicate, but when to communicate effectively to us.

Whenever it is necessary, the Holy Spirit will speak to you. It might seem that He is quiet or not speaking much but trust Him, He will speak at the right moment so that you won't miss a beat on your journey with Jesus. The Psalms declares, "God is our refuge and strength, a very present help in trouble" (Psalm 46:1). It might feel like it is too late and that all is lost, but God has a word for you at the proper moment in time!

> "So don't be misled, my dear brothers and sisters. Whatever is good and perfect is a gift coming down to us from God our Father, who created all the lights in the heavens. He never changes or casts a shifting shadow. He chose to give birth to us by giving us his true word. And we, out of all creation, became his prized possession." (James 1:16-18 NLT)

Let's dial in on that second sentence. The passage says, "Whatever is good and perfect." That man that you claim to be in love with...is he good for you? That woman that you claim is "the one"...is she good for you? Are they abusive, vindictive and leading you to sin? If so, they aren't good for you! Every good gift is from God. If it isn't good in your life, it isn't God in your life. If something is harming you, it is on assignment from hell in your life. The word good in this passage means:

- Useful
- Pleasant
- Agreeable
- Joyful
- Upright
- Honorable

This litmus test will save you from making crazy mistakes! Is the person you are dating useful to God, pleasant to the Lord, and agreeable to be with? Are they joyful, upright, and honorable? Is the door you are about to walk through pleasant and righteous? Is it good for you? Will the results be good for you? Will the decision produce good, both in the short term and long term?

On the same line of thinking, we should ask, what does the word 'perfect' mean in the verse above? It means:

- Complete
- Integrity
- Mature
- Virtuous

That business partner that you've been considering partnering with...do they have integrity? Are they God fearing? Is God pleased with them? Or are their standards and convictions low? Do they speak terrible about others? Does God want you in business with that kind of person?

Come on, saints! I've been there. I've walked through the wrong doors before. I've forged ahead with decisions that put me in the room with that which was not good and perfect. It isn't worth it. I believe that God will save you from going through that wrong door! When I've taught these things, I've gotten reports from all over the world of people being rescued from the wrong decisions. They have been rescued from trusting the wrong people or from buying the wrong house. The Holy Ghost will do the same for you.

> "But if ye have bitter envying and strife in your hearts, glory not, and lie not against the truth. This wisdom descendeth not from above, but is earthly, sensual, devilish." (James 3:14-15)

Based on this, you can also tell that it's not of God if there is envy, strife, fleshly, worldly and giving no consideration to convictions and the word of God. This word devilish means resembling or proceeding from an evil spirit. I worked for a company that was involved in lying and ripping people off. I left. I was out. Why? Because I refuse to lie. I refuse to be deceptive. I wouldn't be a part of things that were earthly, sensual and devilish.

I was a technician and I would show up at people's homes. They would say, "Do I need to buy this and that?" They had already been told that they needed to buy all of these things in order to have a proper system. I would say, "No you don't need that at all. Let me just turn this on and get it going for you." The company had called them ahead of time and lied about all the things they needed to buy. I wouldn't participate. I would not lie just so the company could make more money.

> "For where envying and strife is, there is confusion and every evil work." (James 3:16)

Confusion sets in when people begin to yield to the enemy. I had someone write to me recently and they said, "Pastor Sean, I allowed someone to come stay in my house. Ever since they moved in, they've caused headache and strife." My answer? Show them the door! Cast them out of the house and strife will cease. It's not worth it. Protect the peace and the atmosphere of your home.

Have you ever had someone come to your home to visit and after they left it was like a tornado came through your house? This is not of God. You cannot trust that type of person. You must remove this from your household and from your life. Otherwise, you invite confusion and demonic forces that literally block and inhibit your ability to hear from God like you were meant to. Let's continue:

> "But the wisdom that is from above is first pure, then peaceable, gentle, and easy to be entreated, full of

mercy and good fruits, without partiality, and without hypocrisy. And the fruit of righteousness is sown in peace of them that make peace." (James 3:17-18)

Does the situation in your life match this description? If so, you know where it came from: the Lord. Is one job offering you a big paycheck but with it you must lie, cheat and steal? While the other is an integrity-filled company with a more modest paycheck? You ought to know as a believer to choose the path of peace, purity, and life! We are motivated by this in decision making.

"Shew me thy ways, O Lord; teach me thy paths. Lead me in thy truth, and teach me: for thou art the God of my salvation; on thee do I wait all the day." (Psalm 25:4-5)

God is about to pull this verse off in your life. He will do great things. He will lead you in truth. He will highlight which door to open and which job to take. You may have to walk through the door with a lesser offering because of the peace that comes with it. Sometimes God will give you more when you're first willing to take less. He is trying to rescue you from something, are you hearing it?

"Lead me, O Lord, in thy righteousness because of mine enemies; make thy way straight before my face." (Psalm 8:5)

THE FRUIT OF OPEN DOORS

I remember in 1994, God spoke to me that He would open a door for me to go to Bible school. A year later, two doors were in front of me. Both were Christian Bible colleges. I thought, how in the world will I know which one I need to attend?

I prayed about it. I said, "Lord, let the right Bible school be the first to call me and let it work out and fall into place." Within two days that Bible school called me. They sent all of my paperwork, they accepted me, and not only that, they said, "We also have a church that is willing to pay for your tuition." I got my student visa to come to the USA. In fact, there were hundreds of other people in front of me who got denied. Yet when I went to the embassy, the man looked at me, smiled, and stamped the approval. When it is from God, you will have peace about it, like I did, and sure enough—everything will fall into place.

I'm so glad that I walked through that door. When I went to the orientation on the first day, I saw a beautiful young woman. (I didn't go to college to find a woman.) However, I saw this beautiful girl. It was the first time I saw my wife, Aimee. Two years later, we were married and we've been happily married for over 20 years since! We now have 7 beautiful kids and a wonderful life!

Friends, when you walk through the right door, God will blow your mind. Walk through the door that has peace and is free of strife and confusion. Walk through the door that has purity and God's presence. Let the Holy Ghost confirm it through the written word. He loves you. He is for you. He desires to lead you!

10

THE DANGER OF A DEAF EAR

IN THIS LIFE, YOU WILL ENCOUNTER TROUBLE. JESUS promised it when He said, "In the world ye shall have tribulation" (John 16:33). However, you need to know that some troubles can be avoided. I've gone through avoidable trouble and suffered great loss in my life. You don't have to do this! I want to share a biblical account of great loss being suffered from a lack of attentiveness to the Spirit's leading:

> "And said unto them, Sirs, I perceive that this voyage will be with hurt and much damage, not only of the lading and ship, but also of our lives." (Acts 27:10)

The word perceive here is Paul perceiving what the Holy Spirit is saying to him. He was relaying to them a warning that disaster would come. Unfortunately, Paul was a prisoner with no ultimate authority to make the call.

> "Nevertheless the centurion believed the master and the owner of the ship, more than those things which were spoken by Paul. And because the haven was not commodious to winter in, the more part advised to depart thence also, if by any means they might attain to Phenice, and there to winter; which is an haven of Crete, and lieth toward the south west and north west. And when the south wind blew softly, supposing that they had obtained their purpose, loosing thence, they sailed close by Crete." (Acts 27:11-13)

Notice, outwardly everything looked fine. People thought it would be best to move ahead. The passage even states that, "the wind blew softly." I grew up in the Bahamas and I know how nice that soft wind can be. The seas are calm and glassy, the weather is perfect. Yet, you must remember, we don't move forward by outward circumstances. We move forward by the Spirit's leading.

> "But not long after there arose against it a tempestuous wind, called Euroclydon." (Acts 27:14)

They were basically caught up in a hurricane. Now, when they first loosed to go, everything was fine. Yet the Holy Spirit in Paul knew what was to come. Many times, I've been on airplanes and I sense in my spirit that turbulence is coming. I began to pray in tongues and bind the storm and sure enough a few minutes later the pilot comes on the intercom and says, "Buckle up, we are about to experience turbulence." God will prepare us for storms that are approaching!

In this story, the storm became so bad that it lasted for more than two weeks. They started throwing everything off of the ship. The storm cost them their cargo and luggage. Cloud cover caused them to lose their ability to see the stars which was their GPS in that day and age. In this storm, Paul speaks up:

> "And when neither sun nor stars in many days appeared, and no small tempest lay on us, all hope that we should be saved was then taken away. But after long abstinence Paul stood forth in the midst of them, and said, Sirs, ye should have hearkened unto me, and not have loosed from Crete, and to have gained this harm and loss." (Acts 27:20-21)

In other words, Paul says, "I told you so." Yet he doesn't leave it here! He continues to preach:

> "And now I exhort you to be of good cheer: for there shall be no loss of any man's life among you, but of the ship. For there stood by me this night the angel of God, whose I am, and whom I serve, Saying, Fear not, Paul; thou must be brought before Caesar: and, lo, God hath given thee all them that sail with thee.

Wherefore, sirs, be of good cheer: for I believe God, that it shall be even as it was told me." (Acts 27:22-25)

I've been like the captain of the ship and ignored the warning of the Holy Spirit coming through genuine men and women of God. As a result I have suffered great losses. I certainly was guilty and brought that upon myself and had to repent and ask God to forgive me and He did. I still had to deal with the consequences of my decision.

Of course God is merciful and gracious when we repent and will bring us out of our mess. On the other hand, I've also been in Paul's position where I did not bring it on myself but it was the result of those I had no control over, like the captain of the ship. The captain's decision to forge ahead and ignore Paul put the life of everyone on the ship in danger.

You might have been forced into a situation like Paul, and had no final say in the decision to move forward. A storm has risen as a result. Yet God hasn't left you. Just as Paul said, so you can say, "I believe God, that it will be just as it was told me." You can be of good cheer for you will make it through the storm!

You must believe God just as it was told you in scripture. Believe God just as it was told you in your spirit! After Paul announced these things the scripture goes on to say, "And the rest, some on boards, and some on broken pieces of the ship. And so it came to pass, that they escaped all safe to land." (Acts 27:44)

You will make your escape to safety! You will get out of the storm, because you didn't bring this upon yourself. The voice of the Lord tried to get them to not set sail yet they did. Then the voice of God through an angelic visitation pulled them out of the mess when God's servant, Paul, stood up and spoke up!

When you read stories like this, it is no wonder that Paul cried out, "If God be for us, who can be against us?" (See Romans 8) Likewise, in your life, you might have gone through storms and situations because of the decisions of other people but God wants you to know in the midst of it all He will bring you out victorious.

11

BETTER TO BE SAFE THAN SORRY

WITH THIS BOOK, I WANT YOU TO BE ABLE TO RECOGNIZE when an inclination is the voice of the Spirit, the voice of your flesh, or the voice of the devil. Many people have all three manifesting in their mind yet they have no clue how to discern the difference between them. The Bible says, "There are, it may be, so many kinds of voices in the world..." (1 Corinthians 14:10). You've got to know which is which.

Guessing is not God's will. You don't have to be questioning, nail-biting, and wondering about the will of God. If you position yourself in prayer, God will speak to you. He wants to! You don't have to beg. He wants to communicate with you.

I hear many people beg and cry out to God, "Oh Lord I want to hear your audible voice." Listen, you don't have to beg God to hear His voice and especially to hear His audible voice. The scripture states that you will hear the voice of God but it does not state that you will hear the audible voice of God.

We get into error when we read about an encounter with scripture or we hear a testimony from someone else and we pin God down to a specific method or means of speaking and manifesting. It's unsafe to only accept a sensational, audible experience. Can God move in those ways? Certainly! Yet it doesn't mean that He always will. In fact, God won't fit inside of your box and often will move in ways beyond your expectation.

Our job is to simply approach in faith, and trust that the Lord will get His message across to us. Paul said, "For we walk by faith, not by sight" (2 Corinthians 5:7). We don't live by sensations, audible sounds, and experiences. We live by and through faith in the word of God and the God of the word!

DIVINE REPETITION

When God speaks a thing to us, He is sure to get His message across loud and clear. Often, He does so through repetition. When God wants to emphasize a matter, He often repeats that matter.

> "God hath spoken once; twice have I heard this; that power belongeth unto God." (Psalm 62:11)

In other words, when God speaks to you, you will hear it more than once. He will speak once, and then continue to bring it back to you over and over and over again. God will repeat Himself and continue to remind, prod, nudge, and encourage you with His instruction. He comes peacefully and taps you on the shoulder. He doesn't bring a dark presence and nasty spirit. No, that's the devil. God speaks peacefully with His instruction and love. That's why when God gets ahold of us, we suddenly begin to stream tears down our faces, we lift our hands, and celebrate His loving faithfulness.

Why does God speak repeatedly? Because He wants to convince you! He wants you to be fully assured that His word has been confirmed in you! Paul alluded to these realities in his second letter to the Corinthians:

> "This is the third time I am coming to you. In the mouth of two or three witnesses shall every word be established." (2 Corinthians 13:1)

This means that if someone prophesies something over you, you can expect that if it is of God, it will be confirmed in two or three alternative, independent ways. Perhaps someone lays hands on you and speaks a word over you, then you go home and are reading the Bible and that same principle pops off the page at you, then later on in a different meeting in another town an independent person approaches you and utters similar things over you. This is an example of repetition and confirmation which is a proper and safe way to know that something is of God.

> "Whom shall he teach knowledge? and whom shall he make to understand doctrine? them that are weaned from the milk, and drawn from the breasts. For precept must be upon precept, precept upon precept; line upon line, line upon line; here a little, there a little." (Isaiah 28:9-10)

Just recently, God was giving us direction in our lives. As we've spent time alone with God, studying and meditating on the word, certain things kept coming back over and over again. God was stacking His rhema truths to us precept upon precept and line upon line. Then we turned on a message from a trusted, reliable man of God and as he preached his message, he went into the exact scriptures that we had been hearing God speak to us that week. He literally went through each point and principle that we had been immersed in. We see this same sort of repetitious speaking in Acts:

> "I'm completely in the dark about what will happen when I get there. I do know that it won't be any picnic, for the Holy Spirit has let me know repeatedly and clearly that there are hard times and imprisonment ahead." (Acts 20:23 MSG)

Notice the wording, the Holy Spirit let Paul know repeatedly and clearly that hard times and persecution were coming. It wasn't a one-off word from God. It was a continual outpouring of the voice of God in this area of his life! Paul would show up to a city and a man of God would prophesy over him, confirming the same things.

In 1993 when I first got saved, I would spend time in the prayer closet and hearing from God in His word, as I still do. As I read Jeremiah 1, God confirmed His calling on my life to me. I felt that God was calling me in the same way that He called Jeremiah. It was so clear. It was like the word jumped off the page and was imparted to my spirit. A week after that, I went to a meeting in the Bahamas and a genuine, known prophetess was speaking. She stood up in the middle of the service and called me up. She said, "God spoke to me and wanted me to tell you that just as He called Jeremiah, He is calling you!" I jumped up and had a Holy Ghost fit. I leapt, shouted and cried. It confirmed everything that I had heard in the secret place.

A few weeks after that, I was at another service and a mentor of mine, who didn't know what God was speaking to me in private and didn't hear the previous lady's prophecy said to me, "Brother, God has spoken to me to tell you that just as He called Jeremiah, He is calling you!" Again I wept and fell out in the spirit, completely undone under the power of God.

Yet again, a few weeks after that, I was in a service and an Apostle of God stood up and the spirit of prophecy came over him. Sure enough, when he got to me he said, "Young man lift your hands up to heaven. The Lord says, 'Just as I called Jeremiah, so I am calling you!'" God is not confused! He knows just what to say to you! He knows just how to confirm it. He will lead you by the word of God and confirm it by a man or woman of God.

God will solidify that which He has spoken to you, often through repetition from varying sources. He will repeat it and make it clear. You don't have to beg for someone to prophesy over you. I get people who write to me all the time and say, "Pastor Sean, can you prophesy over me?" Yes! I've got a prophecy for you: go study to show yourself approved. Go read your Bible! Go spend time in prayer and seek the face of God!

Stop looking for shortcuts! God lives in you! As we've described in this book, "Know ye not that ye are the temple of God, and that the Spirit of God dwelleth in you?" (1 Corinthians 3:16). Paul also said, "To whom God would make known what is the riches of the glory of this mystery among the Gentiles; which is Christ in you, the hope of glory" (Colossians 1:27). Have a look at that final phrase, "Christ in you, the hope of glory." The word glory there means, any manifestation or attribute of God displayed in the earth. Do you realize that it's Christ in YOU who will manifest Himself in your life and in the world around you? You don't have to wait on the Christ in someone else!

12

DON'T LOSE HIM!

COMPROMISING IS A DEADLY ENEMY WITH A COSTLY PRICE. You cannot afford to lower your standards on God. Don't play around with sin. Everyone is tempted, but not everyone has to yield to temptation. The Bible says that Jesus was at all points tempted as we have been, yet without sin (see Hebrews 4). He is our example. Everyone is tempted. Don't let the enemy guilt you over being tempted. Yet we don't have to obey a sinful nature. You can overcome sin, the enemy, and temptation. The Holy Spirit exposes the tricks, plots and plans of the enemy.

In Judges 16 we see the renowned story of Samson. When I was a young boy, I used to think that Samson was a strong and mighty man because he had long hair. When I got saved I realized it was the Holy Ghost who made him strong and his long hair was just an act of obedience to walk in that strength. In fact, one thousand

Philistines came against Samson at once. The Spirit came upon him, he took the jaw bone of a donkey and killed 1,000 men. That was the Spirit operating in his life.

No mere man with earthly strength could single-handedly defeat such a group. He also snatched a big heavy gate off of the city walls and walked uphill for several miles with that gate over his head. We also see stories of him tearing apart lions with his own hand and catching foxes and setting their tails on fire. He was able to do superhuman things by the power of God.

However, Samson had a problem. He began to take the anointing for granted and started to flirt with sin. His parents and the Holy Spirit had warned him about women yet he ignored them and got connected with Delilah. It turns out that the leaders of the Philistines were planning to use Delilah to discover the secret of Samson's strength. She cooperated with a seducing spirit and began to wear Samson down.

> "And it came to pass, when she pressed him daily with her words, and urged him, so that his soul was vexed unto death." (Judges 16:6)

Samson should have gotten out of the situation in a hurry but remained with lustful intentions. He was dancing with the devil, so to speak. The chapter goes on to say:

"That he told her all his heart, and said unto her, There hath not come a razor upon mine head; for I have been a Nazarite unto God from my mother's womb: if I be shaven, then my strength will go from me, and I shall become weak, and be like any other man.

And when Delilah saw that he had told her all his heart, she sent and called for the lords of the Philistines, saying, Come up this once, for he hath shewed me all his heart. Then the lords of the Philistines came up unto her, and brought money in their hand. And she made him sleep upon her knees; and she called for a man, and she caused him to shave off the seven locks of his head; and she began to afflict him, and his strength went from him." (Judges 16:17-19)

Just like that, the man with supernatural strength lost his might. His disobedience grieved the Holy Spirit. He thought that he could remain in compromise and continue with God's strength. Yet this wasn't so and he found out soon after:

"And she said, The Philistines be upon thee, Samson. And he awoke out of his sleep, and said, I will go out as at other times before, and shake myself. And he wist not that the Lord was departed from him." (Judges 16:20)

He said, "I will go out as at other times, and shake myself." Friends, you cannot shake yourself free. You cannot break the bonds of sin and oppression on your own. It requires the help of God. And tragically, in this case, Samson relied on the flesh and only received from the flesh—which was no help to him at all. God had left him. The Spirit departed. When this happened, he became weak. Look at the next verse:

> "But the Philistines took him, and put out his eyes, and brought him down to Gaza, and bound him with fetters of brass; and he did grind in the prison house."
> (Judges 16:21)

They mocked him, belittled him, blinded him and imprisoned him. There is such danger in losing the Holy Ghost! The word tells us not to grieve the Spirit. He is a person, He lives in you. You cannot just do whatever you want with your body. You've been bought with a price and have become the habitation of God. Grieving Him will cause you to become a normal man or a normal woman without anointing and power. I want to tell you, however, that there was redemption available to Samson and redemption is available to you! The word says, "Howbeit the hair of his head began to grow again" (Judges 16:22).

If you're reading this and you've grieved the Spirit and lost the anointing, I want you to know that your hair is beginning to grow back. Your strength is going to come full circle back into your life if you'll repent and get things straight. Later in this story, Samson was put between two pillars during one of the biggest pagan celebrations of that day. He cried out to God and asked for one more chance. He asked to die with those rascals with a final victory.

Sure enough, the anointing came back, his strength returned, and he pushed the pillars apart—collapsing the entire facility and killing more enemies in his death than he did in his entire life previously. It was a type and shadow pointing to Christ who destroyed the enemy with his death.

If you've grieved the Spirit, it's time to turn back. The scripture says, "He that covereth his sins shall not prosper: but whoso confesseth and forsaketh them shall have mercy" (Proverbs 28:13). Don't cover it, defend it, or hide from it. *Fess up when you mess up* and stay with the Holy Ghost!

Throughout this book we discuss hearing the voice of the Spirit and it goes without saying, should the Spirit leave you—His voice will depart as well. Sensitivity to His voice will keep you away from compromise and sin. As a result, His voice will remain and continue in your midst. It's a dangerous world outside of the Spirit's presence. Our job is to learn from what Samson did wrong and avoid those same mistakes, while also observing what he did right and duplicating those same principles.

13

KING DAVID'S GREATEST FEAR

YOU KNOW THAT DAVID WAS A MIGHTY MAN OF GOD, SO IF there was something that David was afraid of, it should catch your attention. See, David came to the throne after the fall of King Saul. Saul disobeyed the commands of the Lord but never genuinely repented. In fact, he came after David in envy and tried to kill him over and over again. Saul was anointed and used mightily by God but because of his persistence in disobedience, God departed from King Saul. Saul couldn't hear from God any longer. Prophets no longer came to him. As a result, the Spirit of God came upon David from that day forward. God had a replacement prepared.

David was a righteous man who led the nation with justice and godliness. Yet we know that he committed a terrible act of wickedness. When he should have been out to battle, he stayed back and wound up laying eyes lustfully on another man's wife. He slept with her, attempted to cover his own sin, and when that didn't work he sent her husband out to battle to be killed. He is guilty of adultery, a cover-up, and the pre-meditated murder of his own soldier. Yet in all of this, the Lord did not leave David like he left Saul. Why? Because David was a quick repenter. He knew he did wrong, confessed it, and got right with God, whereas Saul did not. This is the primary difference between those who walk this Christian life out with success and those who do not. Let's take in the prayer of repentance that David uttered after these atrocities against God and man:

> "Have mercy upon me, O God, according to thy lovingkindness: according unto the multitude of thy tender mercies blot out my transgressions. Wash me thoroughly from mine iniquity, and cleanse me from my sin. For I acknowledge my transgressions: and my sin is ever before me. Against thee, thee only, have I sinned, and done this evil in thy sight: that thou mightest be justified when thou speakest, and be clear when thou judgest. Behold, I was shapen in iniquity; and in sin did my mother conceive me. Behold, thou desirest truth in the inward parts: and in the hidden part thou shalt make me to know wisdom. Purge me with hyssop, and I shall be clean: wash me, and I shall be whiter than snow. Make me to hear joy and gladness; that the bones which thou hast broken may rejoice. Hide thy face from my sins, and blot out all mine iniquities." (Psalm 51:1-9)

You can easily see the contrition, humility and repentance that is pouring out of David. He recognizes his own weakness and acknowledges God's strength and redemptive ability. The next verses in the prayer reveal David's greatest fear:

> "Create in me a clean heart, O God; and renew a right spirit within me. Cast me not away from thy presence; and take not thy holy spirit from me." (Psalm 51:10-11)

David's greatest fear was that the Holy Spirit would be taken from him! He had seen the removal of the Spirit from King Saul and knew it was trouble. He saw the former King turning to the witch of Endor for direction. He knew he would lose his throne and cost himself and the nation greatly without the anointing of God. David genuinely repented. He did what Saul did not. He continued his prayer with, "Restore unto me the joy of thy salvation; and uphold me with thy free spirit" (Psalm 51:12).

God answered the prayer and redeemed these matters. The second child David had with Bathsheba was King Solomon, the wisest and richest king to ever walk the planet. Had David not cried out to God for mercy, these redemptive realities would not have been seen and the history of Israel could have been greatly altered, for the worse.

God is not impressed by the size of the offense. He is impressed and moved by repentance and humility. As we live in this place of repentance, we will find the Spirit remaining with us. We will find mercy and grace in our time of need. The word says, "For a just man falleth seven times, and riseth up again" (Proverbs 24:16). The problem is, many fall down seven times and stay down. Yet our task is to get up eight times if we fall down seven. These practices literally let the voice, presence, power and activity of God loose in our lives. When you avoid repentance, you avoid His voice. When you embrace repentance, you turn up the volume of His voice in your life.

14

CHRIST, THE SPIRIT, AND YOU

IF JESUS TRUSTED THE HOLY GHOST, SO CAN YOU. JESUS could not even come to the earth without the Holy Spirit. Isaiah prophesied about the coming of Christ and said, "Therefore the Lord himself shall give you a sign; Behold, a virgin shall conceive, and bear a son, and shall call his name Immanuel" (Isaiah 7:14). I'm sure for many centuries, folks wondered how this would play out. I want to break down three attributes of Christ's relationship with the Holy Spirit beginning with the first:

1) JESUS WAS CONCEIVED BY THE HOLY SPIRIT

The word says, "Then said Mary unto the angel, How shall this be, seeing I know not a man? And the angel answered and said unto her, The Holy Ghost shall come upon thee, and the power of the Highest shall overshadow thee: therefore also that holy thing which shall be born of thee shall be called the Son of God" (Luke 1:34-35).

The Holy Spirit is the one who made the conception possible in Mary's womb. If Christ's entry into this world was not even possible without the help of the Holy Spirit, how much more do we need the Holy Spirit today? Jesus was born of the Spirit, and we as believers are born of the Spirit.

2) JESUS WAS ANOINTED FOR SERVICE BY THE HOLY SPIRIT

Jesus was empowered to carry out divine service by the Holy Spirit. It took place specifically at the baptism of Jesus and went as follows:

> "And Jesus, when he was baptized, went up straightway out of the water: and, lo, the heavens were opened unto him, and he saw the Spirit of God descending like a dove, and lighting upon him: And lo a voice from heaven, saying, This is my beloved Son, in whom I am well pleased." (Matthew 3:16-17)

It's no surprise that we see this playing out in Matthew 3 as it was prophesied in ages past when Isaiah said, "And there shall come forth a rod out of the stem of Jesse, and a Branch shall grow out of his roots: And the spirit of the Lord shall rest upon him, the spirit of wisdom and understanding, the spirit of counsel and might, the spirit of knowledge and of the fear of the Lord" (Isaiah 11:1-2).

Notice, it is the work of the Spirit to walk in wisdom, understanding, counsel, might, and knowledge. It's the Spirit who produces in us the fear of the Lord. It's a joke to me when folks tell me that they are full of the Holy Ghost but they live like devils. This isn't right! The same attributes of the Spirit that were in Christ will also be in us when we walk in fellowship with Him. We see Christ alluding to this very anointing later in Luke:

> "The Spirit of the Lord is upon me, because he hath anointed me to preach the gospel to the poor; he hath sent me to heal the brokenhearted, to preach deliverance to the captives, and recovering of sight to the blind, to set at liberty them that are bruised." (Luke 4:18)

These are all things that Christ has also commissioned us to take part in. His commission has become ours. His mandate has become ours. His path has become our path by and through the great commission in Mark 16, which says:

> "And he said unto them, Go ye into all the world, and preach the gospel to every creature. He that believeth and is baptized shall be saved; but he that believeth not shall be damned. And these signs shall follow them that believe; In my name shall they cast out

devils; they shall speak with new tongues; They shall take up serpents; and if they drink any deadly thing, it shall not hurt them; they shall lay hands on the sick, and they shall recover." (Mark 16:15-18)

If Christ has called us to do the same things He did, don't you know He has called us to be anointed with the same Spirit He was anointed with? God isn't asking you to do the works of God without the power of God to do so! He isn't asking you to drive on an empty tank. No, He gives the commission and gives the fuel. You are not without the help of the Holy Ghost.

3) JESUS WAS LED BY THE HOLY SPIRIT

"And Jesus being full of the Holy Ghost returned from Jordan, and was led by the Spirit into the wilderness." (Luke 4:1)

"And immediately the spirit driveth him into the wilderness." (Mark 1:12)

We have discussed at length that we as the sons and daughters of the Most High have the same exact ability to be led by the Spirit of God (see Romans 8). In the same way that Jesus was led, step by step by the Spirit, so shall we be led. In fact, Christ declared, "Then answered Jesus and said unto them, Verily, verily, I say unto you, The Son can do nothing of himself, but what he seeth the Father do: for what things soever he doeth, these also doeth the Son likewise" (John 5:19).

Did you catch that? Jesus only did what He saw the Father doing and only said what He heard the Father saying. How did He recognize these things? Through the leading of the Holy Spirit. As adopted children of God we have the same duty and honor to be led to duplicate what Jesus does and says, as we are led by His Spirit.

4) JESUS HEALED THE SICK AND CAST OUT DEVILS BY THE HOLY SPIRIT

"But if I cast out devils by the Spirit of God, then the kingdom of God is come unto you." (Matthew 12:28)

"How God anointed Jesus of Nazareth with the Holy Ghost and with power: who went about doing good, and healing all that were oppressed of the devil; for God was with him." (Acts 10:38)

The anointing and the Spirit were central to the healing ministry of Jesus and the deliverance ministry of Jesus. Without the Spirit, these things would not have happened. There is no division and disunity in the Trinity. The Godhead does not function separately, for our God is one. Christ was in perfect harmony with the Holy Spirit and carried out these wonderful works by Him. When we dive into praying for the sick and casting out devils, we must do so in partnership with the Holy Spirit.

Otherwise, make no mistake about it, our efforts are futile.

5) JESUS RAISED THE DEAD BY THE HOLY SPIRIT

> "When Jesus therefore saw her weeping, and the Jews also weeping which came with her, he groaned in the spirit, and was troubled." (John 11:33)

Notice, He groaned in the Spirit. The Holy Spirit was stirring within Him and getting ready to do something powerful. Jesus knew by the Holy Spirit that something was off with the situation and that God's will would manifest. Let's continue:

> "And when he thus had spoken, he cried with a loud voice, Lazarus, come forth. And he that was dead came forth, bound hand and foot with graveclothes: and his face was bound about with a napkin. Jesus saith unto them, Loose him, and let him go." (John 11:43-44)

Not only did Jesus raise the dead by the power of the Spirit but we see the Apostle's doing the same. We see the same thing happening throughout church history, even up until today. You and I can raise the dead by the Spirit's power.

6) JESUS DIED ON THE CROSS BY THE HOLY SPIRIT

> "How much more shall the blood of Christ, who through the eternal Spirit offered himself without spot to God, purge your conscience from dead works to serve the living God?" (Hebrews 9:14)

How did Jesus offer Himself without spot to God? Through the eternal Spirit. His very death was brought about through the Holy Spirit. It was the Holy Ghost that inspired Him to announce forgiveness to those that were killing Him and it was the Holy Spirit who strengthened Him to go through with the slaughter.

7) JESUS WAS RAISED FROM THE DEAD BY THE HOLY SPIRIT

> "And declared to be the Son of God with power, according to the spirit of holiness, by the resurrection from the dead." (Romans 1:4)

> "But if the Spirit of him that raised Jesus from the dead dwell in you, he that raised up Christ from the dead shall also quicken your mortal bodies by his Spirit that dwelleth in you." (Romans 8:11)

The grand finale was brought about by, you guessed it, the Holy Spirit. From His conception to His life, ministry, and service, even up to His death and triumphant resurrection—it was all empowered and manifested by the Spirit of God.

The Bible says that when the last trumpet blows we all who are righteous in God will be raised up from the dead. How will that happen? By the Holy Spirit of God at work in the earth. The same resurrection power that launched Christ from the tomb dwells in us, not someday but today!

If we are going to be effective Christians and witnesses for God the way the early church was, we have to learn to depend on and cooperate with the Holy Ghost. It's simple: if Christ did it, so shall we. If we neglect the things Christ embraced, we will falter. If we cling to what He clung to, we will experience the blessed purpose and prosperity designed for us.

15

CONCLUSION

HEARING FROM THE HOLY SPIRIT DOES NOT HAVE TO BE AN intimidating thing. A small child is able to hear their parent speaking. Likewise a young believer can hear from the Lord. It doesn't take decades of maturity and experience. It takes a childlike faith and a willing heart. In fact, when you got saved, you heard from God. Jesus declared that one cannot come to Him without the Spirit drawing that person and making the arrangements. The fact that you came to Christ proves that you felt and acted on the leading of the Spirit.

The model by which you continue to be led by the Spirit is the same, with some varying methods, as we covered in this book. I encourage you to explore the voice of the Spirit. Get into your Bible and devour it until a scripture leaps off the page and brands itself into your heart. Let God bring about confirmation through human vessels. Open yourself to His still small voice and subtle impressions. Let the peace of God be your thermometer as you gauge the decisions of life. Don't exempt yourself from His active leading. Thrust yourself into it!

CORRESPONDING CHAPTER QUESTIONS

Chapter 1: The Spirit's Grid

1. In what ways has the Holy Spirit manifested as your parakletos (one alongside you to help)?
2. The chapter mentions that you hear from God more than you realize. Looking back at your life, do you see times when God spoke to you but you didn't realize it? What can you learn from that?
3. In what ways specifically does the Holy Spirit provide light to your path? Are there areas in your life that you need God's light to shine to bring understanding?

Chapter 2: God's Gold Standard

1. Have you ever found yourself lacking the written word of God? What were the effects of this?
2. Why is the Bible the safest way to hear from God?
3. Have you ever used the Bible to decipher if an impression was from God? What did you learn from it?

Chapter 3: Human Vessels

1. How has listening to a sermon or teaching brought encouragement straight from God into your life? How did you know it was God speaking through a person?
2. This chapter mentions that the true voice of God through a person brings comfort, peace, direction, correction, discipline, encouragement, and breakthrough. Have you experienced each of these by God using a person?
3. How can you enjoy the benefits of hearing from God through people while not becoming dependent upon hearing from God through people?

Chapter 4: Heavenly Dreams & Visions

1. Why might God choose to speak visually through visions and dreams? What benefit do these methods offer us?
2. If you have a dream or vision that you believe is from God, what steps can you take to properly steward it?
3. Accountability is so important when handling visions and dreams. What should your response be if a trusted, seasoned pastor informed you that a dream you had was not from the Lord?

Chapter 5: God's Hallmark

1. Many folks have paid heavy prices for ignoring disruptions in their spirit and forging ahead with their plans. Have you? What can you learn from this?
2. What does the peace of God feel like? How specifically can you recognize it on a decision?
3. Why do people bypass the peace of God in search of sensationalism and audible voices? How can you avoid this?

Chapter 6: Divine Impressions

1. What impressions or similitudes have you felt from the Lord lately? What does it mean?
2. Do you ever find it difficult to recognize when something is or is not a God-thought? What steps can you take to tell the difference?
3. How can impressions be useful to you in the arena of ministry to other people?

Chapter 7: Circumstantial Speaking

1. What is the Lord saying through the events in your life right now?
2. We know that God is not speaking through just any and every outward circumstance. Yet sometimes He is. Name some key indicators that reveal God speaking through circumstances.
3. This chapter mentions going with the flow when God is changing your season. Season shifts can be scary. How can you overcome this and stay in God's will?

Chapter 8: The Still Small Voice

1. What distractions have come up in your life, causing you to miss the *still small voice*? How can you thwart these disruptions?

2. What has the still small voice sounded like to you?
3. Paul and Barnabas heard the still small voice when they ministered to the Lord, fasted, and prayed. How specifically do these things position us to receive the voice of the Lord?

Chapter 9: How to Be Sure It's a God Thing

1. What would be an example of a critical moment where one needs to hear the direction of the Lord?
2. Are there things or situations in your life that you've accepted that are not good and perfect, like the scripture states? What is your plan to get rid of these things?
3. What kind of fruit have you seen sprout in your life by being led to the right door?

Chapter 10: The Danger of a Deaf Ear

1. Paul perceived that trouble was ahead but was speaking to people who wouldn't listen. How can you remain tender and encouraged when warning folks that won't listen?
2. Are there avoidable storms that you are watching others walk through? How can you be a redemptive help to them, like Paul was to those on board?

3. Perceiving oncoming trouble is a powerful tool for the believer. In which other examples in scripture could trouble have been avoided? What lessons can you take away from these accounts?

Chapter 11: Better to be Safe than Sorry

1. This chapter states that *guessing* is not God's will. Why is being sure of God's will of such importance? What happens when we are not?
2. When God speaks, He often repeats. This gives us confidence. Have you ever felt unsure about whether or not something was God? How can you solve this?
3. This chapter instructs us to stop searching for shortcuts. What shortcuts to the voice of God are out there that you should avoid?

Chapter 12: Don't Lose Him

1. Samson was consecrated to God from a young age but began flirting with sin. It cost him dearly. In what ways do modern believers flirt with sin and how can it be avoided?
2. If we press our own fleshly ways, we'll experience the anointing lifting from our

lives. Why does this happen? Is it possible to get it back?
3. What did Samson do right? How can you duplicate those things? What did Samson do wrong? How can you avoid those things?

Chapter 13: King David's Greatest Fear

1. Repentance was so crucial to David's success. What has repentance done in your life? How can it lead us to success?
2. David humbly broke before God. What does humility have to do with hearing from the Holy Spirit and receiving from God?
3. Are there sinful areas of your life that you need to confess to God to bring about purging and cleansing?

Chapter 14: Christ, the Spirit, and You

1. This chapter brings out seven ways that Christ was in cooperation with the Spirit. We need this same sort of cooperation yet many avoid the Holy Ghost, even in churches. Why is this and how can it be solved?
2. Have you ever found yourself trying to make it in your own strength? How can you avoid this moving forward?

3. What goals do you have for hearing the voice of God as you move forward in your walk with Jesus?

MEET THE AUTHOR

Pastor Sean has conducted miracle crusades in Freeport, Bahamas; Uganda, Africa; Angamaly and Mala in India; and Mabelvale, Arkansas. He has held miracle services in local churches in several cities throughout America and in the Bahamas. Through social media, Pastor Sean has reached over 235 nations with the gospel and has ministered to several million unique viewers on YouTube resulting in over 247,000 subscribers. Through evangelistic healing crusades, powerful radio and television broadcasts, and the Internet, Pastor Sean has seen God work notable miracles in the lives of people with various ailments.

During twenty years of ministry, Pastor Sean has had hands laid on him by Dr. T.L. Osborn, Evangelist R.W. Schambach, Evangelist Reinhard Bonnke, and Pastor Benny Hinn. On June 25, 2016, Evangelist Sean was honored to be ordained into his next level of ministry by Pastor Benny Hinn.

Today, Sean and Aimee are still a team that continually blesses God's people through anointed preaching of the strong, uncompromised Gospel followed by a demonstration of God's saving, healing and miraculous power.

DISCOVER MORE AT:

🌐 www.seanpinder.net
✉ info@seanpinder.net
Youtube / Sean Pinder

TO CONNECT WITH SEAN VIA MAIL:

SEAN PINDER MINISTRIES
P.O. Box 2726
McKinney TX 75070

FOR BULK BOOK ORDERS VISIT:

🌐 www.tallpinebooks.com